no
MASTER

plan

...things i wish i could tell my 18 year old self

written and illustrated by:

JACQUELINE GIELOW

book design by:

JM JACQUELINE MARIE
CREATIVE
www.jacquelinemariecreative.com

Printed by CreateSpace, An Amazon.com Company
Available on Kindle and other devices

dedicated to:

all those who have
supported my outrageous ideas
over the years

Compliment,
DON'T
· COMPETE ·

Trust Your GUT

DON'T

waste time following boys around

7

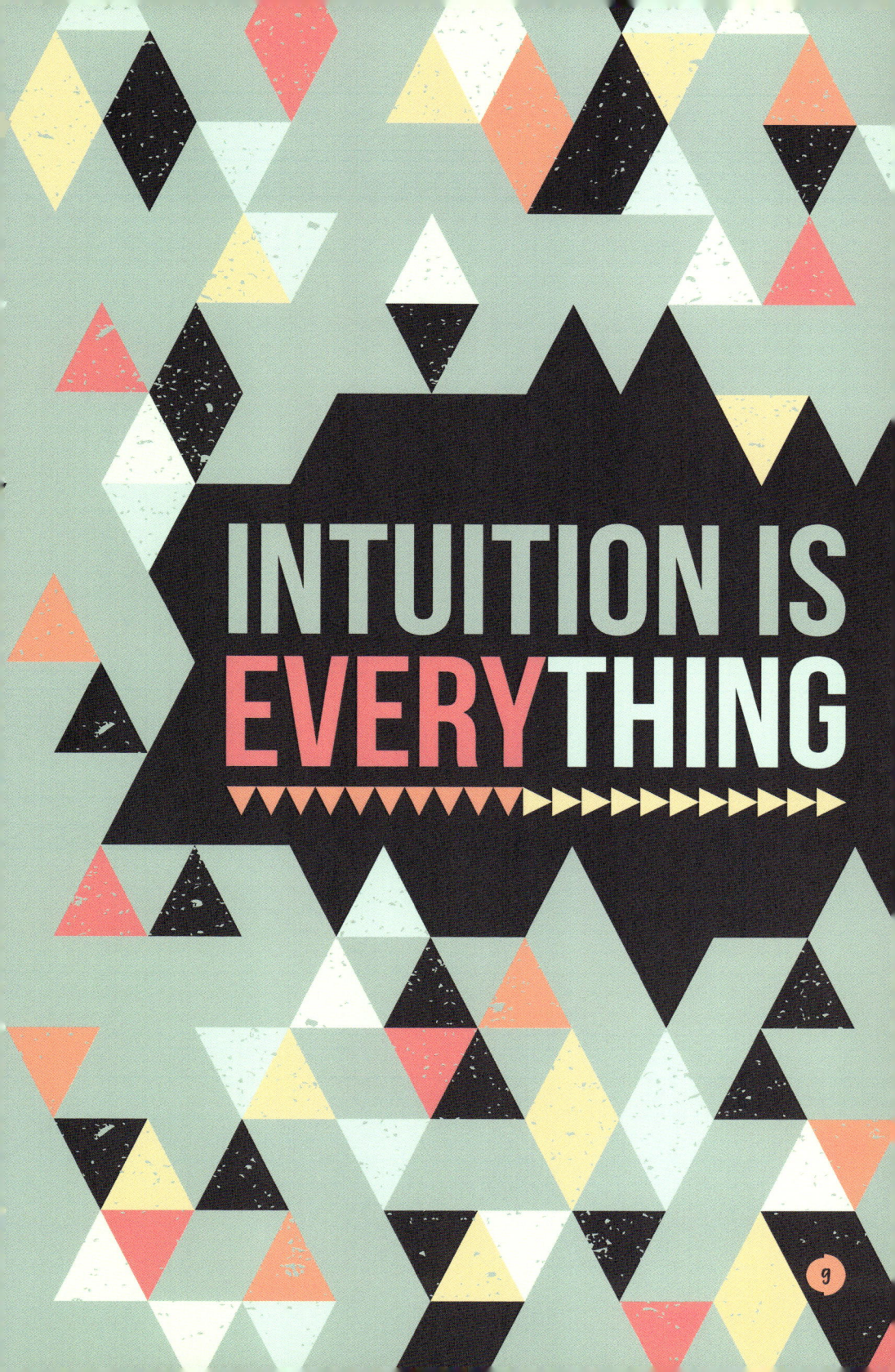

INTUITION IS EVERYTHING

ALWAYS HAVE A BACKUP PLAN

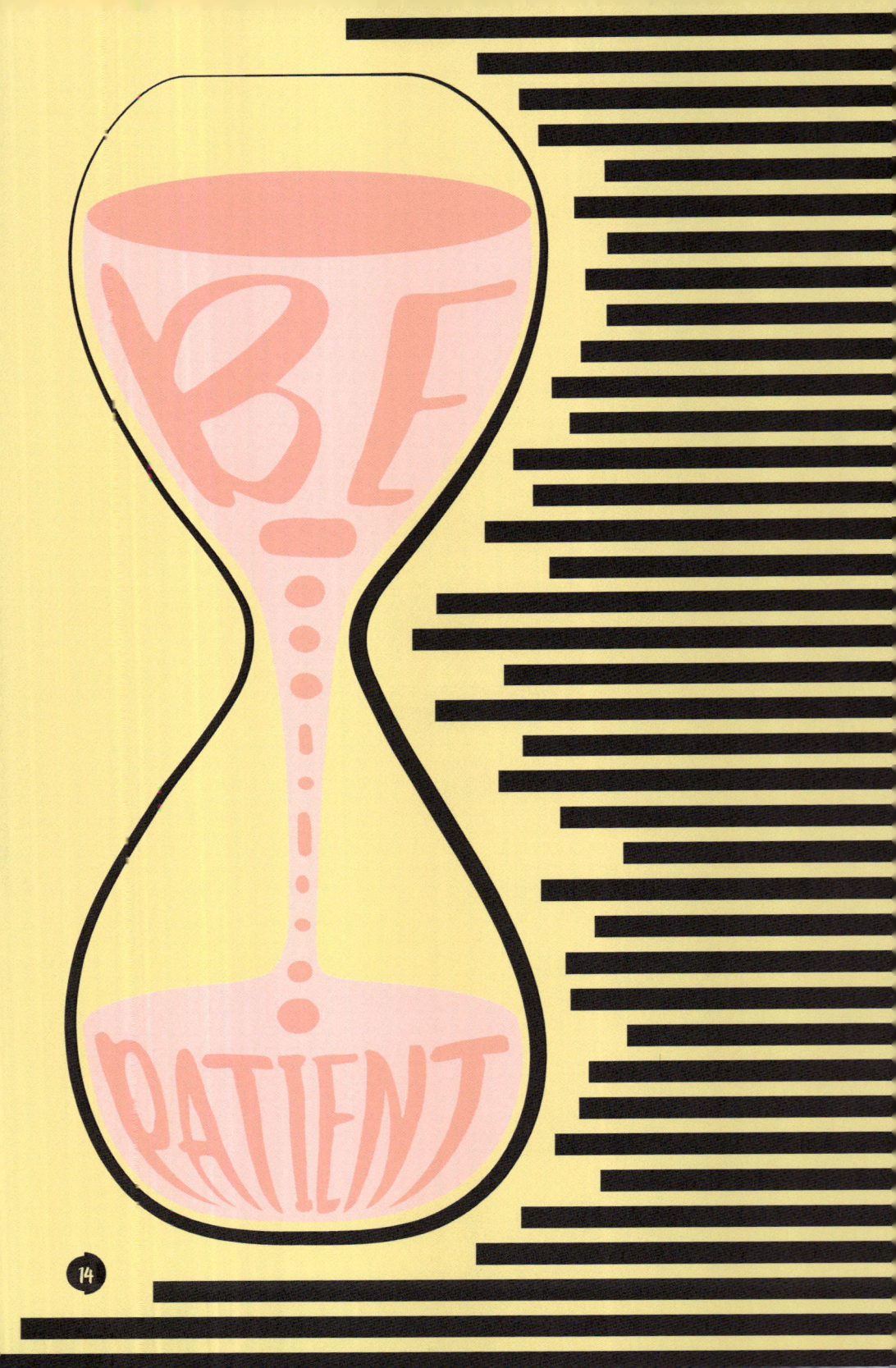

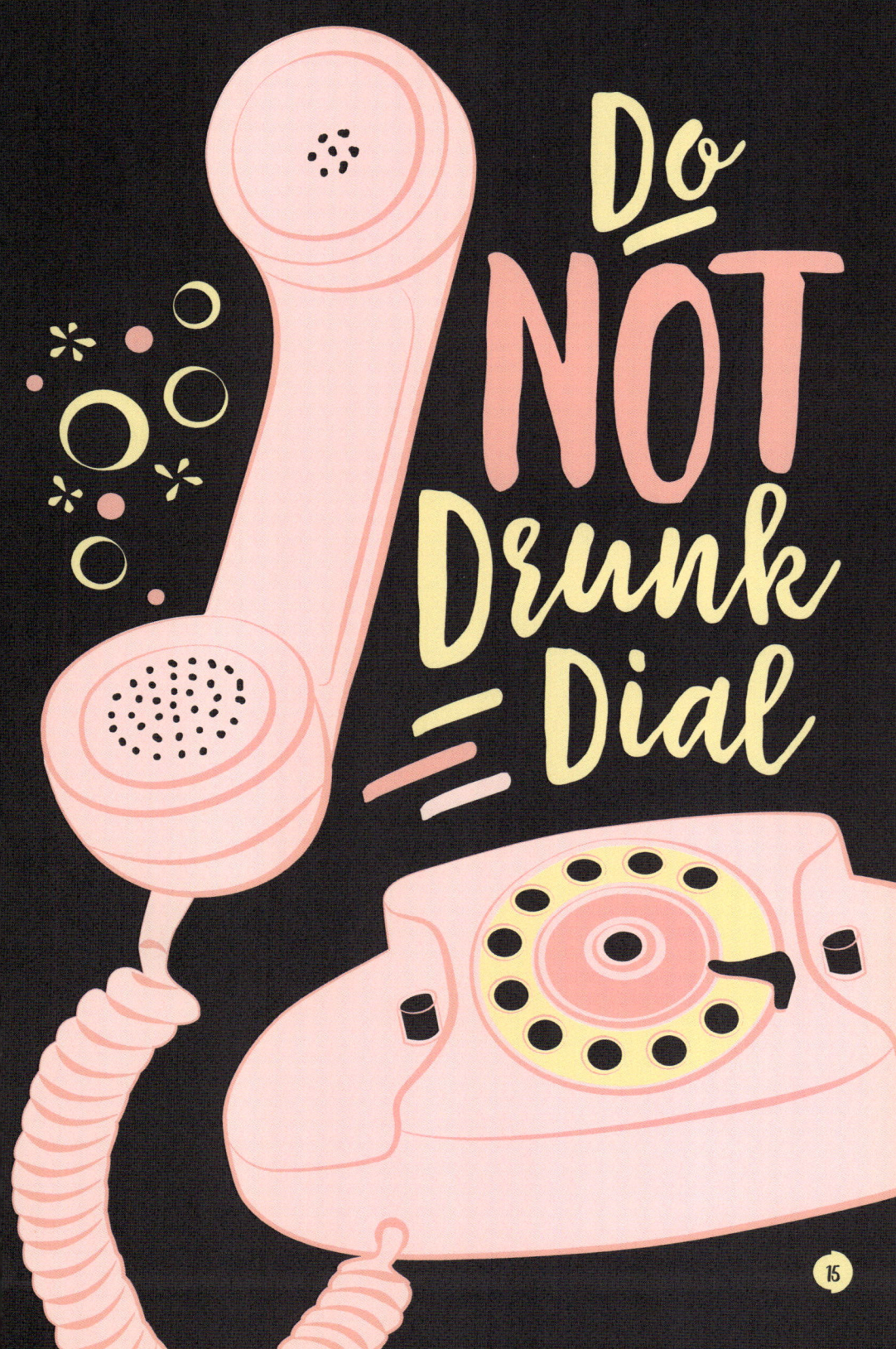

LEAD *don't* FOLLOW

create your own Path

17

YOU'RE NOT OBLIGATED TO KEEP TOXIC PEOPLE AROUND

walk away WHEN THE chase HAS YOU weary

23

Hug tightly

Shake hands

FIRMLY.

25

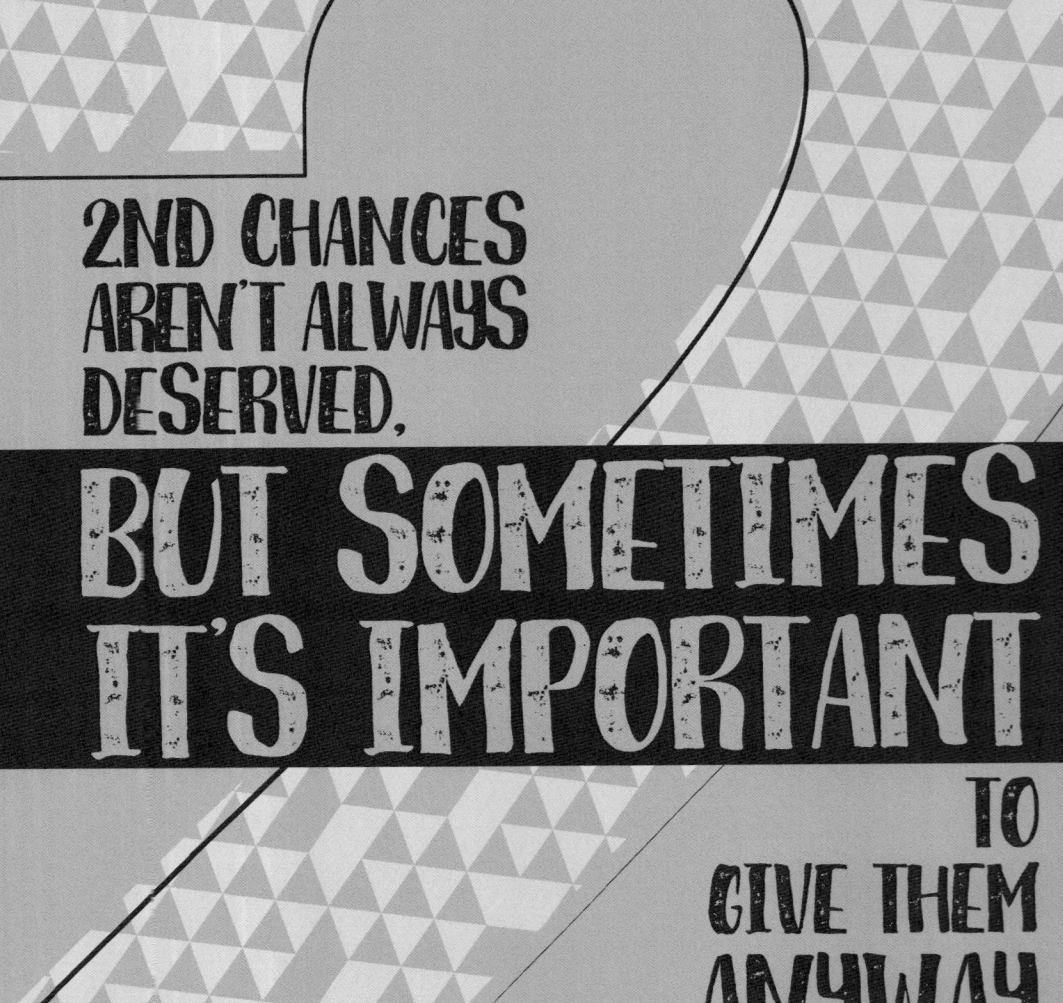

2ND CHANCES AREN'T ALWAYS DESERVED, **BUT SOMETIMES IT'S IMPORTANT** TO GIVE THEM ANYWAY

DO NOT SETTLE *for less than you deserve*

flames
can always be
REIGNITED

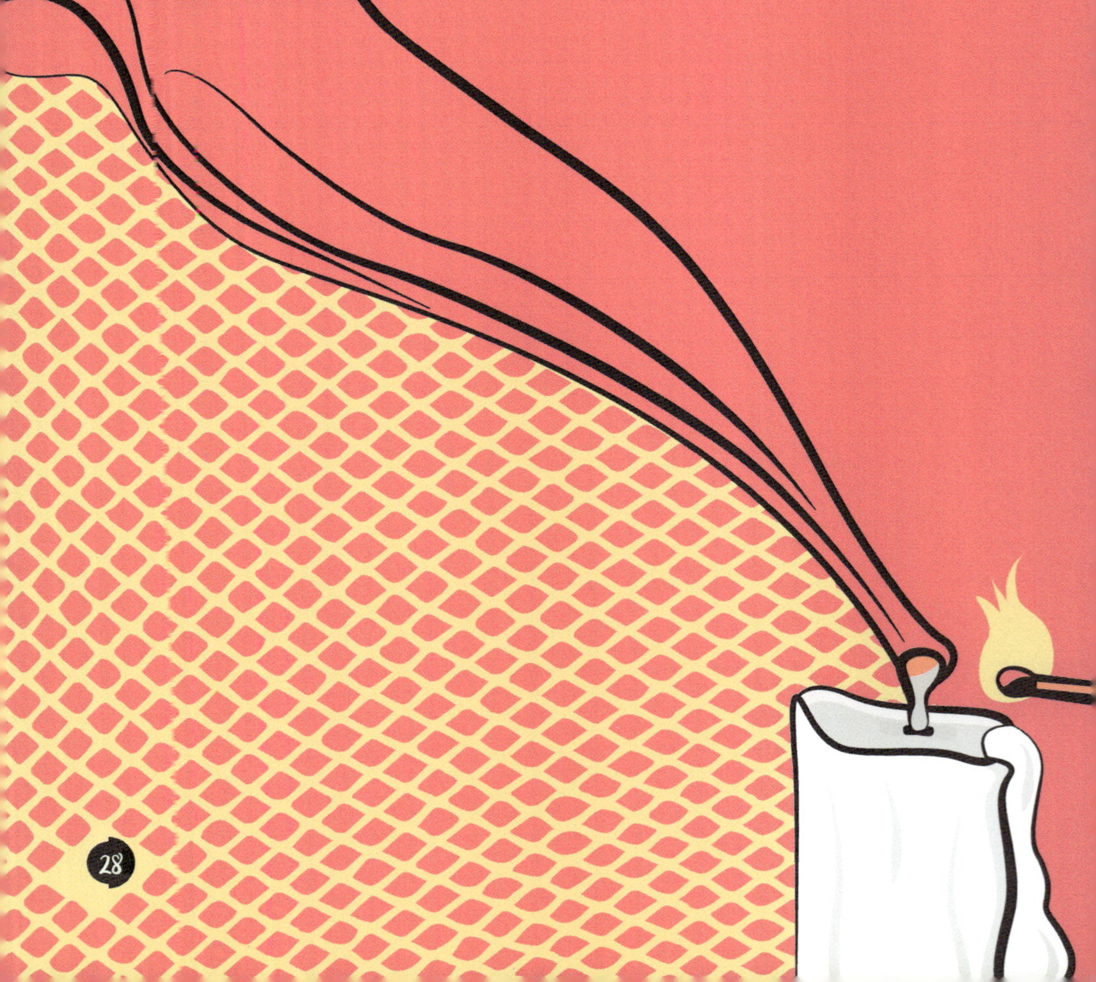

Put it
out into the
universe
and you'll get
an answer

29

FEARLESS

RELENTLESS

NEVER LESS

FIND a Polite WAY TO TELL THE Truth ...ALWAYS.

31

Acknowlege that all people come in many different shapes and sizes

LAUGH IT OFF

HUSTLE

34

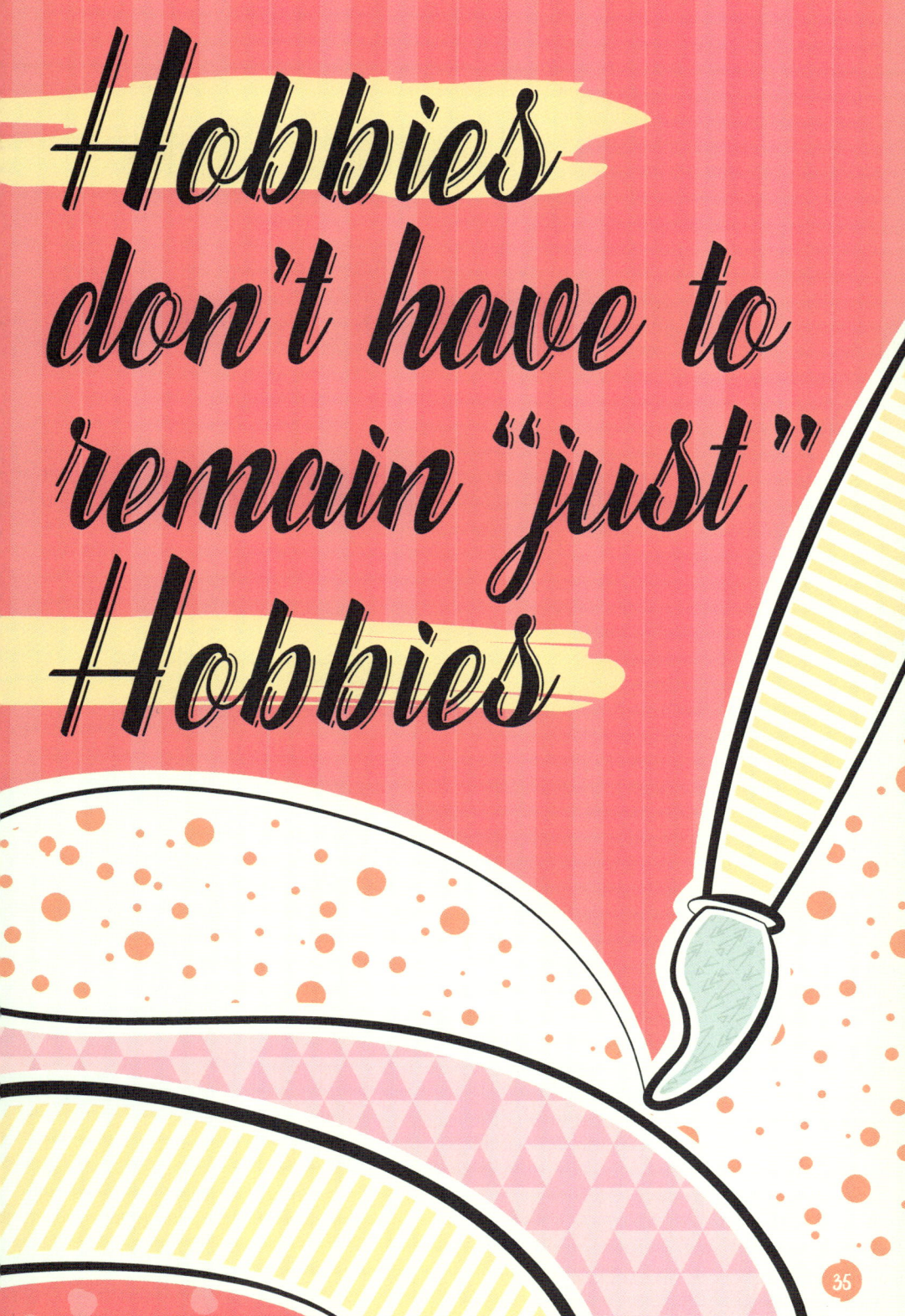

Hobbies don't have to remain "just" Hobbies

35

Let it OUT
&
Let it GO

37

BIG GIRLS DO CRY

it does **not** *mean you are* **Weak**

JU[ST]
BECA[USE]
YOU
DO IT
YOUR [WAY]
DOES[N'T]
MEAN [IT'S]
HAV[E]

40

ST
AUSE
CAN
T BY
SELF,
SN'T
N YOU
E TO

PRACTICE YOGA and BUILD
SELF-AWARENESS

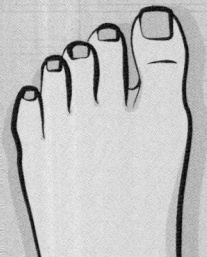
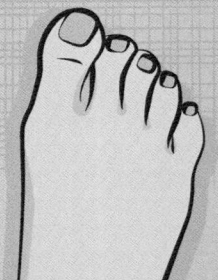

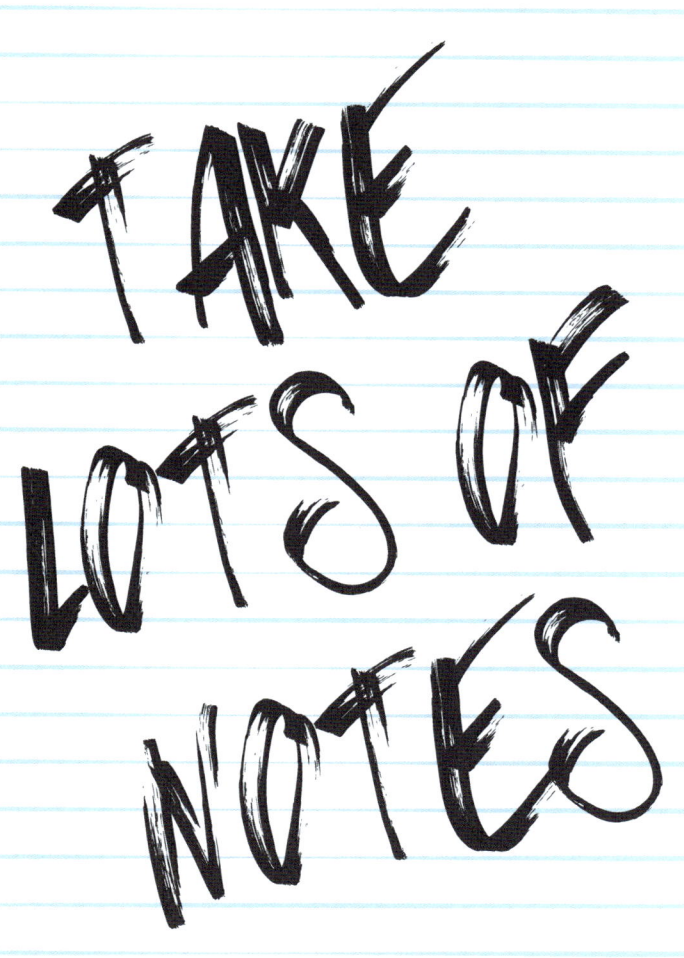

BE ABLE TO PUT YOURSELF IN CHECK

Sex app-eal is not defined by how high your heels are?

47

you can curse if you want to

YOU CAN ALWAYS TEXT
FIRST

....

SEND MESSAGE

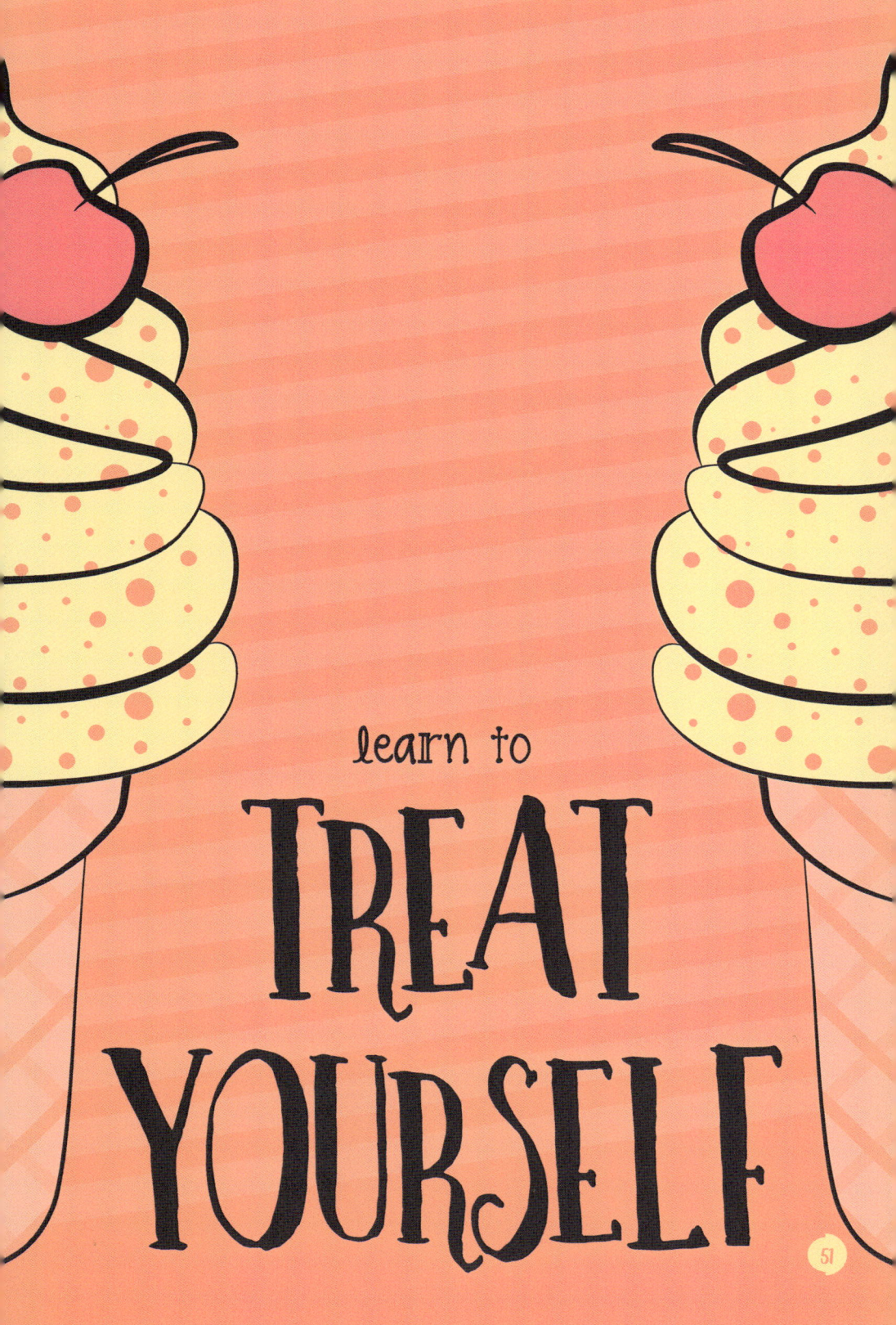

learn to

TREAT YOURSELF

be charitable

DO NOT PERPETUATE

NEGATIVE ENERGY

it is ok to be
TOLERANT

but do not be a
PUSHOVER

Listen to **ALL** DIFFERENT types of Music

have a
Mentor
you trust

the world does not

owe you anything

you will FIND a way

60

GO
DEEPER THAN JUST THE SURFACE

64

LISTEN MORE

TALK LESS

65

Be Humble

You Are Not Always Right

67

DITCH
THINGS
THAT ARE
WEIGHING
YOU
DOWN

learn something new
from everyone you meet

CHOOSE YOUR ROLE MODELS CAREFULLY

you'll get through it all

Do not **OVER THINK** everything

75

learn to SAY you are SORRY

It's not up to you to decide that your problems are more important than the problems of others

Knitting is not just for the elderly

FORM *your* *own* OPINIONS

learn to
Multi-task

THINK

before you

SPEAK

84

you look fine
just how you are

85

TAKE *a deep* BREATH

SAY THINGS ALOUD TO YOURSELF

(they will have a bigger impact)

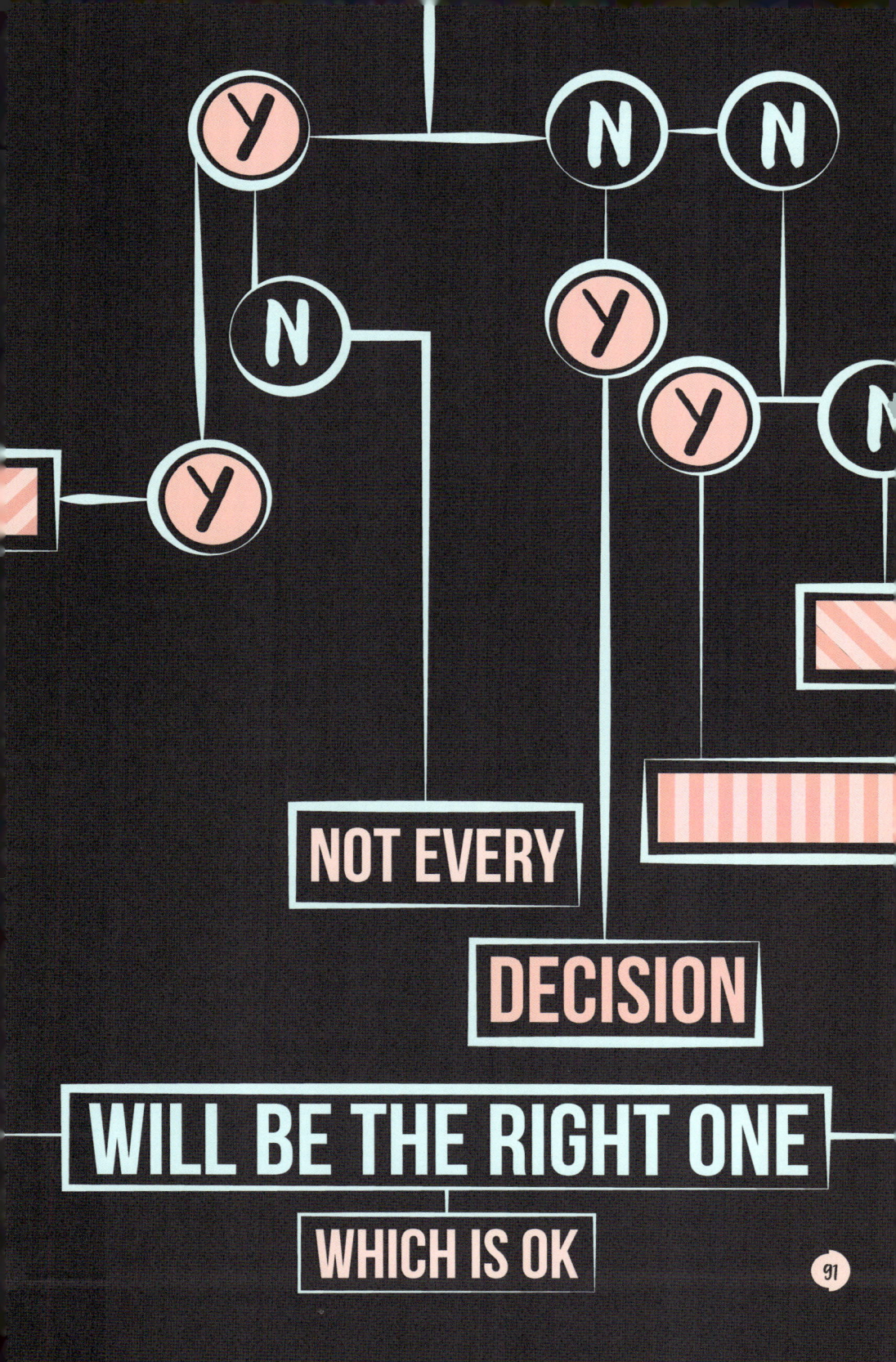

NOT EVERY

DECISION

WILL BE THE RIGHT ONE

WHICH IS OK

GET INTO THE HABIT

1. Shower in the evening so you are not rushed in the morning

2. DON'T let your dirty laundry pile up

3. Rinse off your dishes right away after eating

4. Get plenty of sleep

5. Eat more veggies

6. Laugh Every day

7. Leave early for work or school

8. Follow through when you make a commitment

IF YOU MEET SOMEONE YOU DON'T LIKE, TRY REALLY HARD TO FIND AT LEAST ONE THING YOU CAN APPRECIATE ABOUT THEM

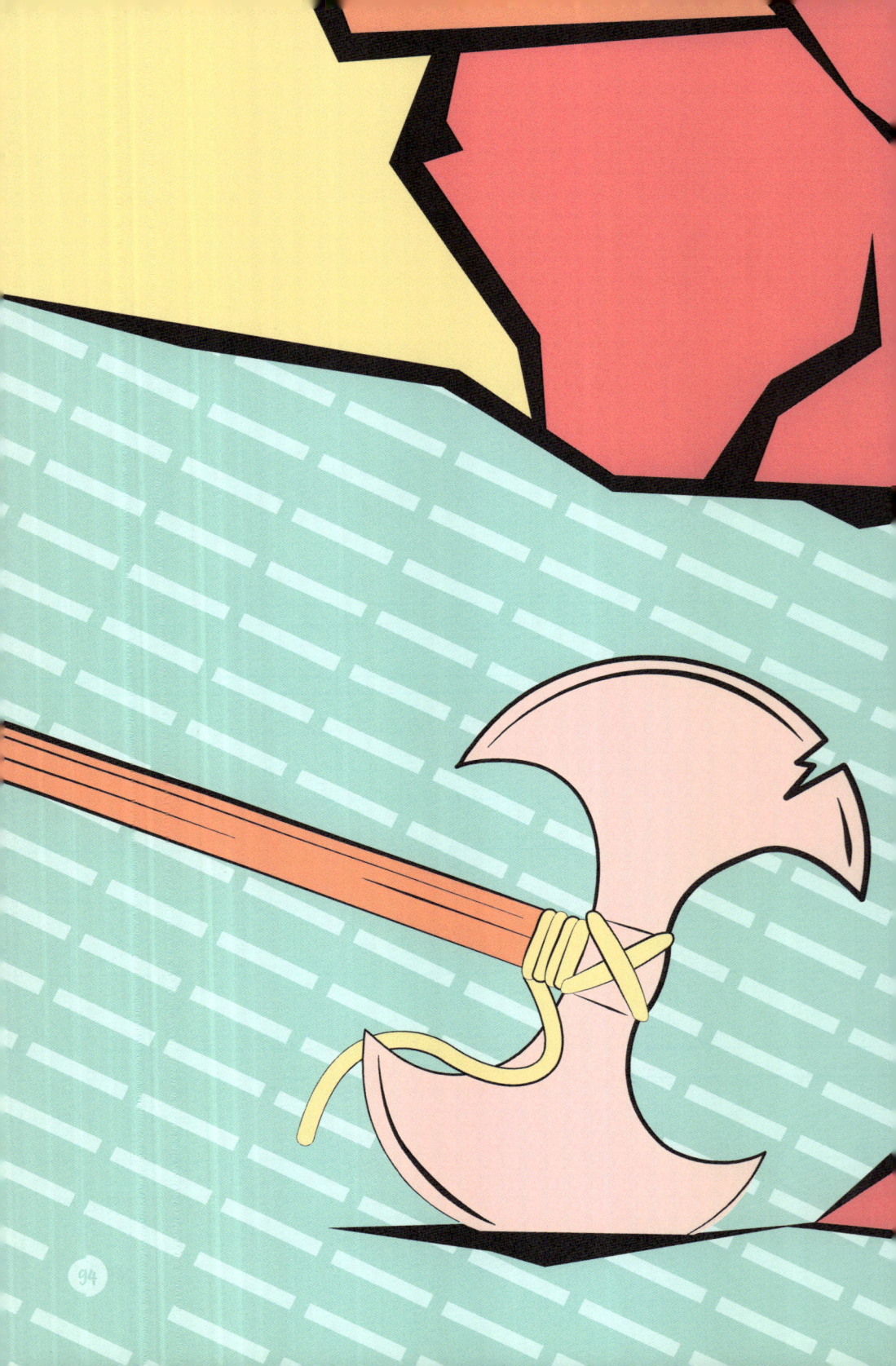

EVERYONE
HAS THEIR
OWN
BATTLES
THEY ARE
FIGHTING

order the ride Home

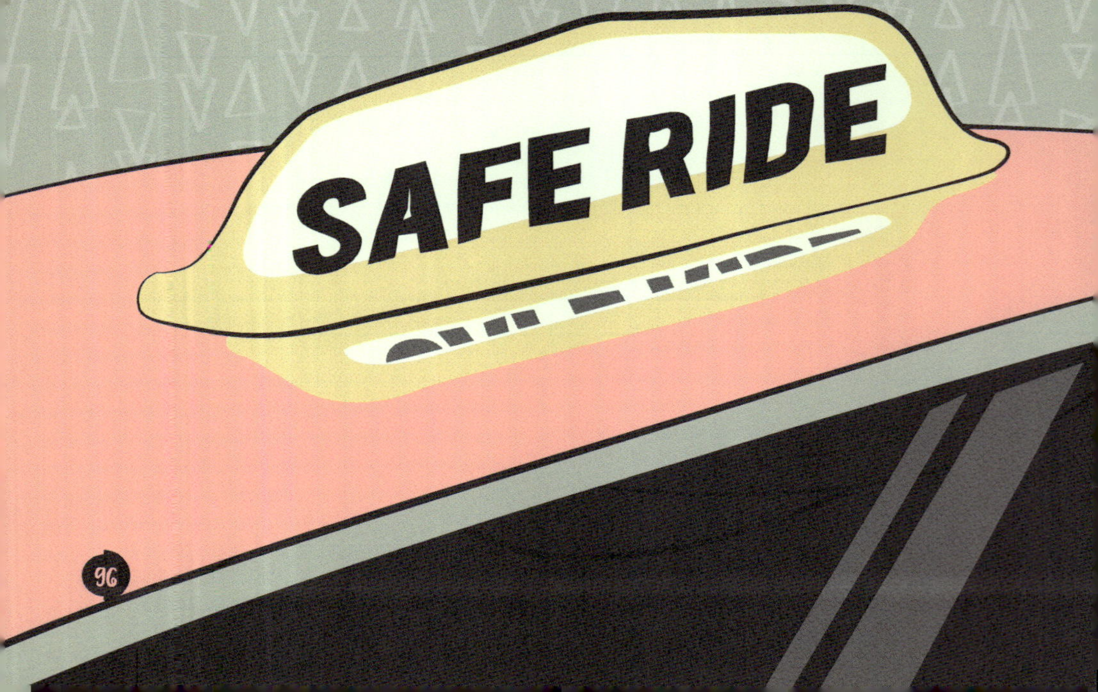

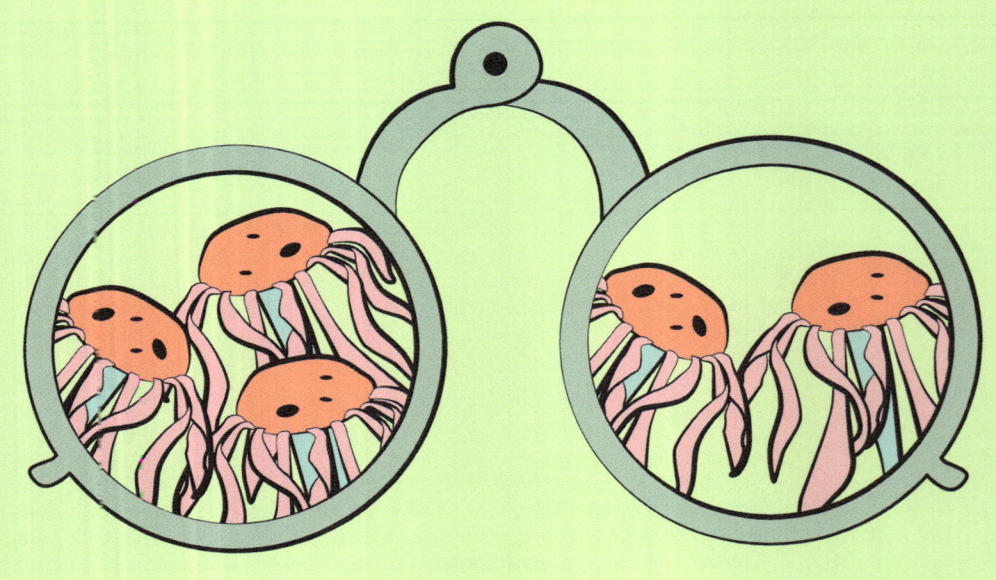

Sometimes you just
have to take another look

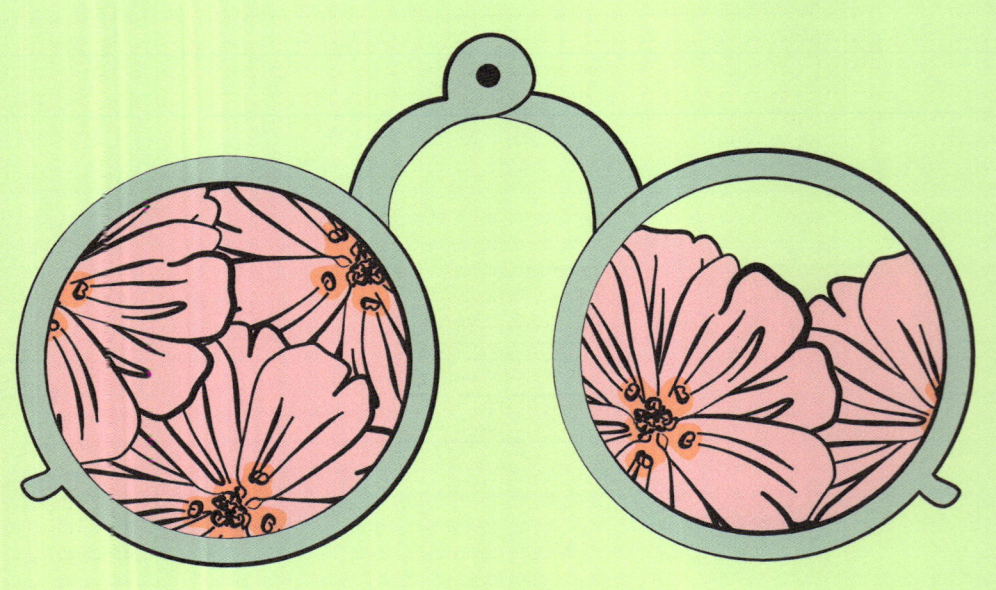

DEFINE YOUR OWN TERMS

YOU CAN MAKE DO WITH WHAT YOU HAVE

• MANY HAVE LESS •

IT IS WHAT IT IS

some feelings will always linger

· BUT ·

you will learn

· to live · with them

104

IF SOMEONE CONFIDES IN YOU,

DON'T BREAK THAT TRUST

106

SOMETHING MISSING?
GO GET IT

108

EM POWER

other women & build them up,
not tear them down

ASK
questions
FIRST

ALWAYS BE AWARE OF YOUR SURROUNDINGS

CHIN UP!

You can do
ANYTHING
you put your mind to

if you stay
committed

...even self publish a book

TIG

Printed in Great Britain
by Amazon